This book belongs to

..............................................................................................................

..............................................................................................................

## Celebrating Differences

"Different, not less." - Temple Grandin.
"Autism is part of who I am" - Anonymous
"Autism is a journey I never planned, but I sure do love my tour guide." - Anonymous.
"Autism is a gift wrapped in a mystery." - Keri Bowers.
"Autism is my superpower, what's yours?" - Anonymous

# Why is he this way?

## Autism at a Glance

Written by Kristy High

Pictures by Zuri Book Pros

Hi, my name is London, and my twin brother Micheal makes me so mad. He always does whatever he wants, he always acts so bad! Dad tells me to be patient, and I try, I swear I do. If you met Michael though, I'd bet you'd be frustrated too. "Michael's just being Michael," seems like it's my mom's favorite thing to say. However, I can't help but wonder why he is this way.

1

I try to be nice to Michael, but he makes it so hard to do. I'm not the only one to notice, the other kids in our class see it too. One time we were at recess in the   middle of a game and Michael ignored all of us any time we said his name.

"Why's your brother acting like that? Why's he being so rude? What did we do to him that he's got an attitude?"

My classmates asked these questions, but I didn't know what to say.

*Michael's just being Michael,* I thought. But why is he this way?

3

Michael's like this all the time, it's not just at school. One time we had to leave the water park early, because he wouldn't stop screaming at the pool. When we go to stores, he's always running everywhere; it doesn't matter if we're in public, Michael doesn't seem to care. Yesterday we went to our aunt's house and Michael wouldn't eat anything. My parents bought Michael pizza on the way home, they treat him like a king!

4

"Why does he get pizza?" I asked. "It's not fair." You want to know the worst part: he didn't even share.

My parents didn't answer the questions, I don't think they knew what to say.

*Michael's just being Michael,* I thought. But why is he this way?

5

Micheal is clearly my parent's favorite even if they won't admit it's true. You'll never believe me when I tell you what they just let him do. Mom was making chili which me and dad like a lot. Michael didn't like it and he dumped out the whole pot!

"What did you do that for?" I asked, trying not to yell.

Micheal just shrugged his shoulders and said he didn't like the smell.

Mom looked annoyed, but she didn't scream or shout. Dad didn't punish Michael except to give him a time-out.  If that had been me, I'd have been in trouble for sure! Dad gave me a whole lecture one time after I slammed a door.

7

"Why is Michael so special; why can he be a brat? Why did you let him get away with doing that?"

My parents didn't answer the questions, I don't think they knew what to say.

*Michael's just being Michael,* I thought. But why is he this way?

"I love Michael," I tell my parents, "But I don't think I like him anymore, and he doesn't like us either, that's one thing I know for sure."

Mom asks me to sit down, dad tells me they have something to say.

"Michael's just being Michael," mom says, "Let us tell you why he's this way."

They tell me Michael has autism, it's a condition related to how his brain works. When Michael acts out, he's not just being a jerk. Sometimes Michael doesn't know how to say what he wants or the right thing to do.

"That must be hard for Michael," I say. My parents tell me it's okay if it's hard for us too.

10

They tell me Micheal is developing differently and doesn't understand some social cues. I ask if that's why sometimes he goes out without his shoes. My parents tell me it's also why he doesn't always share well, doesn't always make eye contact. I think about every mean thing I thought about Michael, and I want to take it back.

"So Michael will get better?" I ask, "He's just not feeling well?" My parents say autism isn't like a cold and only time will tell.

My parents assure me that Michael can learn what's expected. It's important that he feels supported though and is not rejected. I think back to a time in school when Michael sat at his desk rocking. I called him weird then, I didn't stop the other kids from mocking. When my friends asked me what he was doing I didn't know what to say.

*Michael's just being Michael,* I had thought. I didn't know why he was that way.

I ask mom and dad if I can help Micheal learn.

"You've been helping him," I tell them, "Now it's my turn."

"Be patient with your brother," dad says with a smile, "And know if you correct him that it may take a while."

13

"He's sensitive," mom says, "about how things look, smell, and sound, and we don't always know what he doesn't want to be around."

"Can I tell the kids at school?" I ask, "Maybe they'll help too."

My parents say our teacher already knows and that may be a nice thing to do.

14

Things are getting better with Micheal, although he does still sometimes make me mad. Now when he acts out though I know he's not just being bad.

If anyone asks about Micheal now, I know just what to say.

"Michael's just being Michael, he has autism and that's okay!"

# Signs of autism in children

Signs of autism in young children include:

not responding to their name
avoiding eye contact
not smiling when you smile at them
getting very upset if they do not like a certain taste, smell or sound
repetitive movements, such as flapping their hands, flicking their fingers or rocking their body
not talking as much as other children
not doing as much pretend play
repeating the same phrases
Autism in older children

Signs of autism in older children include:

not seeming to understand what others are thinking or feeling
unusual speech, such as repeating phrases and talking 'at' others
liking a strict daily routine and getting very upset if it changes
having a very keen interest in certain subjects or activities
getting very upset if you ask them to do something
finding it hard to make friends or preferring to be on their own
taking things very literally – for example, they may not understand phrases like "break a leg"
finding it hard to say how they feel

Kristy High, M.Ed. is a health and wellness educator with several years' experience working with the pediatric population educating on various health and wellness topics that are prominent today. Kristy has a master's degree in health education with a concentration in health promotion from Virginia Tech. She is passionate about enhancing the knowledge of families and meeting them where they are to assist in improving their quality of life. This book is an introduction to autism, how it can appear in young children, and how it can affect siblings.